The Hermit, the Icon, and the Emperor

The Holy Virgin Comes to Cyprus

by Chrissi Hart ❧ illustrated by Niko Chocheli

CONCILIAR PRESS MINISTRIES ❧ Ben Lomond, California

The Hermit, the Icon, and the Emperor:

The Holy Virgin Comes to Cyprus

Published by Conciliar Press
P.O. Box 76
Ben Lomond, California 95005

Printed in China

ISBN 10: 1-888212-49-7
ISBN 13: 978-1-888212-49-5

Published with the blessing of His Grace,
Metropolitan Nikephoros of Kykkos and Tillyria

Author's dedication:
>   *for my parents, Demetrios and Theodosia Ioannou*

Acknowledgements:
Sincere thanks to my husband Barry for his constant encouragement; professor Annemarie Weyl Carr and Dr. Andreas Jakovljevic for their scholarly assistance, publications, and photographs; Judy Wolfman for her excellent critique; my parish priest, the Very Reverend Father Peter Pier for comments on the early draft; Jane G. Meyer for her excellent editing of the manuscript; Sean Buscay for a fabulous website; Niko Chocheli for his exceptional and beautiful Byzantine artwork; and to our blessed Eleousa of Kykkos, the Merciful Mother of God, for inspiration and guidance.

Illustrator's dedication:
>   *to my beautiful wife Kristen*

Kykkou, Kykkou, Kykkos' hill
A monastery the site shall fill
A golden lady shall enter in
And never shall come out again.

enturies ago, people on the island of Cyprus heard this mysterious song for many days. They heard it all day long, from the time the sun rose until it set. They heard it in the pine forests of the Troodos Mountains. They heard it in the villages of Tillyria and in the Marathasa Valley.

"Who is singing that lilting song?" the villagers asked. "Where is it coming from? What does it mean?" Nobody knew. It was a mystery.

Then one day, some children saw a small brown cuckoo bird high in a tree singing the song. "A singing bird!" they cried. "I don't believe it!" They marveled at its special talent. Everyone talked about the singing cuckoo.

ne morning, Duke Manuel Boutoumites (Voo-too-mi-tis), the governor of Cyprus, went to the pine forest to ride and hunt. He was spending his summer vacation in the Troodos Mountains, where the cool air was better for his health.

Many wild goats, deer, and birds lived in the dense Troodos forest. Soon Boutoumites became lost. "Which way did I come from?" he asked himself. All the paths and trees, shrubs and ferns looked the same.

After wandering through the forest on his horse for several hours, he saw an old hermit monk dressed in rags walking toward him.

"You there," Boutoumites shouted. "Can you tell me the way out of this forest?"

ithout looking up, the hermit kept walking. "Why don't you answer me?" Boutoumites bellowed. "Don't you know who I am? I am the governor, Duke Boutoumites, the emperor's most honored general! How dare you ignore me!"

Still the hermit did not answer. The governor became angrier and shook his clenched fists at him. "You fool. What is wrong with you? Are you stupid?" Boutoumites shouted. He struck the old hermit, who stumbled and fell to the ground.

At last the hermit spoke. "What have I done to deserve this treatment? I am a simple man and do not care for worldly things. Why don't you leave me alone?"

The governor rode away on his horse, leaving the old hermit on the ground. Boutoumites continued to wander around the forest. Eventually, exhausted and weary, he found his way back to the village and his friends.

After a few days, Boutoumites returned to his house in the city of Nicosia and forgot about the old hermit. But the next morning when he awoke, Governor Boutoumites could not move. He couldn't move his arms or his legs. As hard as he tried, he couldn't even lift his head from the pillow.

"What is wrong with me?" Boutoumites wondered. Then he remembered the old hermit and the way he had treated him. "I am being punished," he thought. Then he knew what he must do.

Over the next few days, the governor had nothing but time to think and pray. He felt ashamed of his behavior toward the hermit. Boutoumites sent for his servants. "Go find the old hermit in the Troodos Mountains. I need to ask his forgiveness."

eanwhile, the Holy Virgin appeared to the hermit in a dream. "What happened between you and the governor is part of God's divine plan. You must ask him for my icon painted by the Evangelist Luke. Bring it from the imperial palace at Constantinople to Cyprus. It is God's wish as well as mine."

After searching through the Troodos Mountains for several days, the governor's servants found the hermit in a cave. "The governor has asked us to bring you to him," they said.

"I have been waiting for you," the hermit replied. They traveled to the city, where the governor waited anxiously for their arrival.

"My friend," Boutoumites said to the hermit, "I treated you badly. I am truly sorry, and I ask your forgiveness."

The hermit knelt beside him and prayed with all his strength. "O Christ our God, through the prayers of the Theotokos, have mercy on this sick man and heal him. Amen."

Slowly, Boutoumites lifted his head for the first time in days. Then he moved his arms and legs. He sat up and shouted, "I am well again! Praise the Lord!" Turning to the hermit, he said, "Thank you for what you have done for me. I will reward you with money and gifts. But forgive me, I don't even know your name."

t is Isaiah," the hermit said, "but I am not interested in money or possessions. However, there is one thing that you can do for me. There is an icon of the Holy Virgin in the imperial palace at Constantinople that was painted by the Evangelist Luke. It is God's will that you should bring it to Cyprus."

"That is impossible!" exclaimed Boutoumites. "The emperor would never give away such a treasure!"

"If you want to be forgiven, you should do as the Mother of God asks," the hermit replied.

Boutoumites thought about Isaiah's words and agreed to do as he asked. "I will leave tomorrow," he promised. "But you must come with me."

he next day, Isaiah and Boutoumites sailed over the clear blue Sea of Marmara to the magnificent city of Constantinople. As they approached the city, they could see the imperial palace and the great Church of Saint Sophia.

Luxurious boats painted gold or emerald green sat in the waters. Isaiah stared with awe and amazement at the golden roofs and domes of the palaces and the hundreds of churches, which glittered against the blue sky under the brilliant summer sun.

All around them were chapels, monuments, statues, and pavilions among vines, cypress, olive, and fig trees. There were falling streams, fountains, and gardens of brightly colored, sweet-smelling flowers and herbs.

The gate of the great palace was permeated by the smell of perfume from bazaars that stretched along the main street close by. Isaiah had never seen so many people!

When they entered the great palace, they saw mosaics, treasures, and jewels, works of art, icons, and sacred relics of the saints. They proceeded to the throne room, where the emperor received his guests.

saiah and Boutoumites knelt before Emperor Alexios, who was dressed in purple robes decorated with large gold flowers and braid. A gold crown studded with pearls and jewels sat on his head. Precious stones hung down from the crown on either side of his cheeks. The emperor looked majestic on his golden throne with its purple velvet-covered arms. But his face was troubled, and his dark eyes filled with tears.

"Your Majesty, I bring greetings from Cyprus. But why do you look so sad?" Boutoumites asked.

"My beloved young daughter, the Princess Anna, is extremely ill and has been for a year," he said. "She cannot move her arms or legs. Our best doctors are not able to help. They believe she will die. The empress is with the princess day and night, fasting, praying, and weeping."

"My dear emperor," Boutoumites said, "I had the same illness, and if it wasn't for Isaiah, the holy monk standing beside me, I would still be paralyzed. It is God's will that you should give the icon of the Holy Virgin to Cyprus. Then your daughter will be cured."

"I will do anything for my daughter," the emperor said desperately. "If you can cure her, you may take the icon to Cyprus."

Isaiah stepped forward. "Your Majesty, take me to the icon of the Holy Virgin so I may pray for the princess."

The emperor led them to a small chapel. The icon sat on a jeweled throne, surrounded by embroidered silk veils. Isaiah lit a candle and reverenced the icon of the Holy Virgin. He then fell to his knees and prayed with all his soul.

"O most Holy, Blessed Mother of God, have mercy on the princess and save her through your prayers. Glory to the Father and to the Son and to the Holy Spirit. Amen."

After praying quietly, Isaiah stood up. "Let us go to the princess now and see how she is."

The princess's face was pale against her dark braided hair. As Isaiah made the sign of the cross over her body, she opened her eyes and smiled. Color returned to her cheeks, and she sat up.

"I dreamed of a beautiful bright lady with a golden sun around her head!" the princess said.

"My precious daughter!" the emperor exclaimed, pulling her to his chest. The empress made the sign of the cross and cried tears of joy. At last, their beloved daughter was well again!

saiah knelt before the emperor and reminded him of the icon of the Holy Virgin.

"Give me a few days to get the royal boat ready," the emperor said. "Meanwhile, please stay here at the palace as our guests."

However, the emperor did not want to part with his treasure. Now that his daughter was well, he quickly forgot about his promise. He thought of a devious plan and ordered a famous artist to paint a copy of the icon. "I will send the copy to Cyprus and keep the original for myself," he thought.

Soon after his decision, the emperor was confined to his bed, unable to move, for several days. The Mother of God appeared to him in a dream and spoke sternly to him. "You did not keep your promise. You must send the original icon to Cyprus and retain the copy for yourself."

Only then did the emperor realize that everything that had taken place was indeed God's will. "I have been punished for not keeping my promise," he thought. "And now I must do as I said. Forgive me, Immaculate Lady Theotokos."

The emperor summoned his servants. "Let the monk Isaiah and my friend Boutoumites know that the holy icon is going to Cyprus tomorrow. Decorate the royal boat with colorful and fragrant flowers." And with those words, the emperor's illness miraculously left his body. He wrote his promise with purple ink and sealed the paper with his royal golden seal.

The next day, Isaiah and Boutoumites followed the royal procession along a route strewn with roses, lilies, laurel, and rosemary. The princess kissed the icon of the Holy Virgin and thanked Isaiah for his special prayers.

"The Holy Virgin held this icon in her hands," the princess said to Isaiah.

"Yes, she did," he replied with a smile.

The emperor carefully put the icon, covered with a heavy veil, into the boat.

"I will send money to you to build a church and monastery so the icon will have a home," the emperor said. He handed the *chrysobull*, a royal paper with a golden seal, to Isaiah.

saiah and Boutoumites sailed with the icon
to Cyprus, where the people awaited its
coming. As the boat landed, nature itself
participated in the welcoming celebrations.
The clear turquoise waters stirred. Seashells
and starfish miraculously floated out of the sea in
a sparkling mist, gleaming in the sunshine like
precious jewels.

Isaiah held the sacred icon high in the air with great joy and led the procession, with the seashells following him, from the shore to the Troodos Mountains. The people followed Isaiah with awe and wonder, and great love and reverence for the holy icon.

Holding candles in their hands, the people chanted the beautiful Angelic Hymn. They threw rose petals along the procession route, chanting, "True Theotokos, we magnify you."

The icon is beautiful!" the children exclaimed. They laughed and skipped behind the seashells, trying to catch them in their hands. "See the Panayia's red-and-gold veil!"

"Watch the seashells, they are dancing!" they cried.

"Look at those trees!" they yelled as the pine trees bowed their trunks and branches in great reverence to the holy icon. To this day, the bowed pine trees and seashells remain in the forest regions of Tillyria as an eternal reminder of this wondrous and divine celebration.

At the top of Kykkos' hill, Isaiah placed a cross. "This is where the church and monastery will be," he announced.

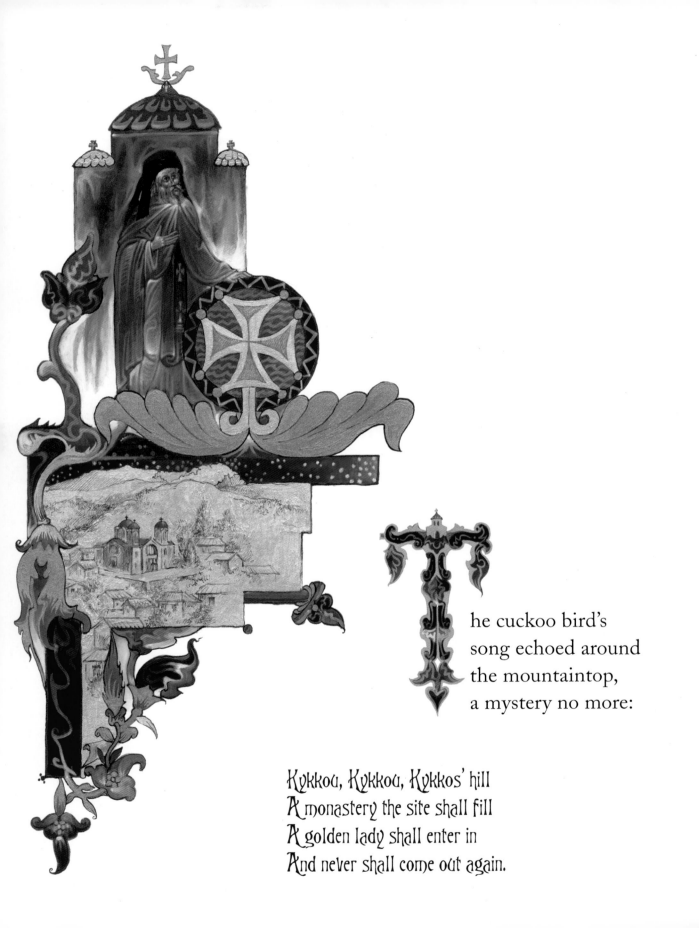

he cuckoo bird's song echoed around the mountaintop, a mystery no more:

Kykkou, Kykkou, Kykkos' hill
A monastery the site shall fill
A golden lady shall enter in
And never shall come out again.

Historical Note

Saint Luke was an apostle, evangelist, physician, and artist. He was born in Antioch, the son of Greek parents. He wrote the Gospel that bears his name and the Book of the Acts of the Apostles, and became the first iconographer. Saint Luke was the first to paint the images of the Holy Virgin and the Lord Jesus, at the request of the Mother of God herself and the main apostles. The *Eleousa*, which means "merciful Mother of God," is one of three original icons painted by Saint Luke.

According to legend, the Archangel Gabriel gave Saint Luke the boards on which the icons were painted. The Holy Virgin held and blessed these icons when she said, "The grace of the One born of me be with them through me." For this reason, the Eleousa is believed to be grace-filled and is dearly loved.

The miracle-working silver-covered icon of the Eleousa of Kykkos hangs on the icon screen at the Holy Monastery of Kykkos in Cyprus. It is also known as the Panagia of Kykkos and the *Kykkotissa*, and is famous throughout the Orthodox world for answering prayers for rain in times of drought and for protecting sailors.

The dynamic image of the Eleousa of Kykkos, with the Holy Virgin's distinctive crimson veil and the barefooted, kicking Christ Child held on her left arm, has been replicated many times over hundreds of years. Since the mid-eighteenth century, the holy faces of the Christ Child and the Virgin Mary have been hidden from view, possibly to inspire more reverence.

Each year on September 8, the Orthodox Church celebrates the birth of the Theotokos, and on October 18 she commemorates Saint Luke.

About the Author

Chrissi Hart was born in Cyprus, grew up in England from age three, and writes stories for children from her cultural heritage that are inspiring and spiritually satisfying. She lives in York, Pennsylvania, with her husband and children. Chrissi's first children's picture book, *Under the Grapevine: A Miracle by Saint Kendeas of Cyprus,* was published by Conciliar Press in 2006. Learn more about her work by visiting www.chrissihart.com.

About the Illustrator

Niko Chocheli was born in Tbilisi, Georgia, and graduated with honors from Tbilisi Nikoladze Art College and the Tbilisi State Academy of Fine Art. He was given permanent residency status by the US government as an Alien of Extraordinary Abilities. His art is often compared to the Great Masters and has received numerous awards. He lives with his wife Kristen in Doylestown, Pennsylvania, where he runs his own art school. Niko has illustrated several Orthodox children's books, including *The Book of Jonah, The Praises,* and *Prepare O Bethlehem!*

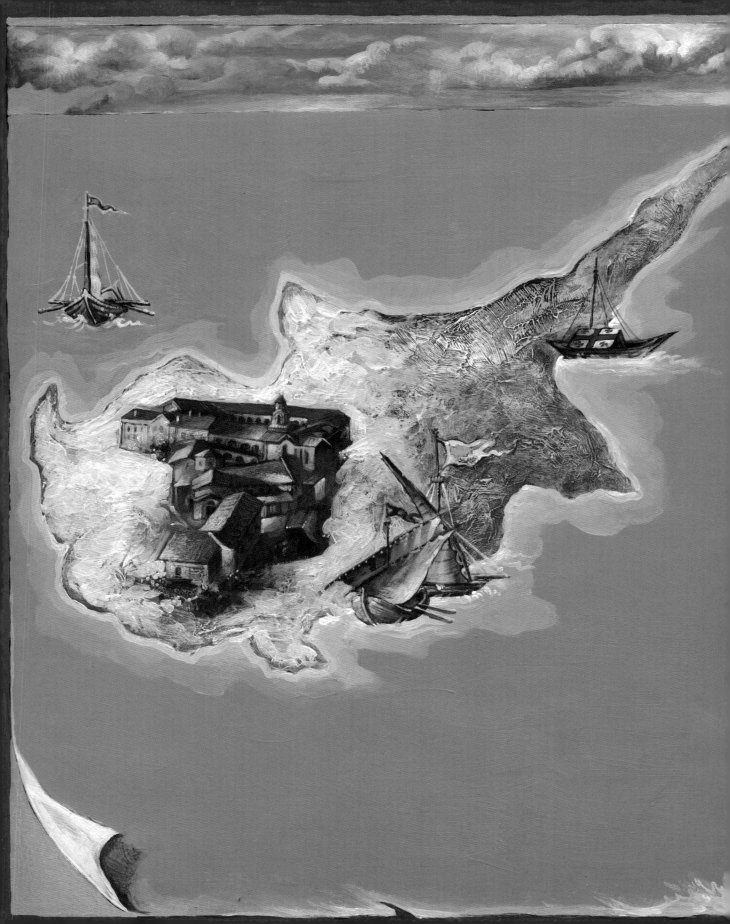